LETTERS TO MY GIRLS

REMEMBER DADDY LOVES YOU

BY: EDVIN E. RUSTRIAN

Author: Edvin Rustrian
Editor: Eli Gonzalez
Book Cover Design and Publisher: The Ghost Publishing, LLC.

Paperback ISBN - 13: 979-8-9854365-5-6

FOREWORD

As I read this book for the first time, I thought, *Every daughter needs to read it.* By the time I finished, I thought, *Every child needs to read this book. Every parent should have this book on their bookshelf.* Edvin Rustrian is one of the great minds of our generation. As pastor of the church that he attends I have been impressed with his heart for his family, his love for God, his commitment to ministry, and his gifting in so many areas.

In the times we live in, we see so much need, failures within homes, families struggling just to stay together, and a disconnect between parents and children. Today, young parents need mentoring and direction like never before. Many parents deal with various circumstances for which they are unprepared. Edvin's letters prepare us in advance for circumstances, emotions, and outcomes that we would have never expected.

As you begin to read each one of the letters you will notice that he addresses his two girls. It soon becomes evident that what he writes originates from the core of his heart. Edvin Rustrian writes from a place of experience. As he inserts his life's story throughout the letters you take part in his journey and how it has prepared him for the great task of writing this book.

I am also a father of girls and, as I read this book I thought, *I need to be more intentional with regards to how I pray for my daughters.* This book is more than just leading us to pray for our children, it will give us direction on how to walk with them during the fragile times of their lives.

I promise you that this book will change the way you pray for your loved ones and change the way you walk with them as well. It will enlighten you with regards to areas of life that are crucial, and if not handled well - can be devasting.

Each chapter is finished with a prayer. I would recommend that you stop there for your reading of the day and let the chapter resonate with you. I know the Holy Spirit will enlighten you and give you discernment to those whom you pray for and awaken things within you that need realignment.

Carlos Medina
Senior Pastor
Elohim Christian Church

Testimonial: Letters to My Girls

Edvin writes a wonderful, tender, loving, warm letter to his daughters. Every man should love their little girls or the girls God places in their lives as Edvin communicates this in his book. Our world is desperate for men who love, protect, and lead their daughters the way Edvin does in this book. He is honest about the struggles and heartaches they will encounter, but he firmly communicates that God loves them even more than he does and has a plan to not only help them through but makes them into the young ladies He designed and created them to be. I highly recommend this book for everyone, but especially Dads who may need a reminder of the influence they have on their little girls' (and their mothers') lives.

Rev. Dr. John Letterman Jr.

Letters of Contents

INTRODUCTION

"Spoken words leave impressions. Printed words leave tracks."

NAPOLEON HILL

My dearest Peanut and Chiqui,

How I long to hold you in my arms again. How I've asked for time to stop then stand still so I might gaze at your beauty and embrace your sweet scent. When you were babies, I would stand by your crib and watch you deep in slumber. You slept and rested as if you were dreaming of chatting with angels in lavish gardens while prancing around exuberantly.

I saw such innocence, such peace within you. Your joy was incomparable. Occasionally, a sweet smile would come across your tiny lips as if something made you laugh or you'd been caught up in the awe and wonder of your creator. Oh, how I love you, my dearest girls. Oh, how I prayed and thanked God every day for the precious gift of your lives. You changed my life, transformed my heart, and gave me a greater reason and purpose to live. God saw that I needed beauty in my life, so He sent you both to me.

There is so much I would like to share with you, so many treasures and pearls I desire to give and impart into your lives. When you were babies, I realized that I could never expect you to remain infants, or even children. I knew that eventually you would grow and blossom into beautiful flowers.

And with those thoughts came many questions and to be honest, fear. The promises I made the very second you were born as I held you in my arms will be put to the test. I hope that, as a loving father, I will uphold the greatest virtue of all, *courage*. As I held newborn babes in my arms, I made the following promises: I promised that I would never let anything bad happen to you, I promised to protect you from all threats and evil, I promised to be there for every event in your life, I promised to play princess games and have teatime with you. I promised to tell you bedtime stories and pray with you every night. I promised to scare away the monster in the closet or under the bed, I promised to buy a big house with many rooms so you can jump and play in each one. I promised you that I will always be there to listen, care and help you when you need me most.

The truth is, I have been able to keep some of those promises, but not all. The reason is that life is quite unpredictable, and I could never keep you from experiencing the pain one feels from a wounded heart. I could never numb your heart from the pain of losing a friend or when life's unbearable storms destroy all your dreams. I couldn't prevent disappointment and setbacks and failures that tormented your minds and dissuaded you from the path you desired to walk. When discouragement knocks at your door and invites itself to walk alongside you, reminding you that you will never accomplish your dreams, know that I am there but cannot sway your discouragement.

It's for those reasons and more, that I desire to leave with you these letters you can read when those tough moments arrive on your doorstep. These letters will remind you that Daddy loves you, always have, always will. I hope that as you read each letter you will hear my voice just as if we might be sitting on the sofa or at the dinner table or in your room talking for hours 'till tears flowed down our cheeks. I hope you will see my heart through each word as I share pearls and jewels that will serve as a guide through the storms of life, so you can anchor your life on principles that will birth great joy, peace, wealth, health, honor, and virtue. The following letters will contain the essence and treasures of my heart which I have discovered through the odyssey of life and saved for you.

Remember,
Daddy loves you.

My prayer,

My heavenly Father, I pray that you provide me the wisdom, knowledge, and meticulous care to leave words that will serve my daughters as a guide, so they can pull from in time of doubt or much-needed assurance. I pray you watch over them and be their Shepherd as they traverse through life's toughest terrains. I pray the counsel provided will draw them to think of how critical and essential it is to walk with the Prince of Peace, Christ Jesus our Lord. Amen.

Who Am I?

"See what great love the Father has lavished on us, that we should be called children of God. And that is what we are!"

1 JOHN 3:1 NIV

My dearest Peanut and Chiqui,

How I long to be near you to see your smile. As you read this letter, I want you to ask this question, *Who am I?* This is a question that humanity has asked for thousands of years. For centuries, this question has been at the forefront of the human heart, its purpose, and its quest for identity and meaning. Consequently, today so many people spend money, time, and energy in self-discovery seeking to find a sort of magical, mystical, or supernatural awakening that will lead them to their next best life. As commendable and admirable as this thought is, it quite often leads many people away from their intrinsic value and worth.

There are a few things I would like to share with you on this topic of identity and the question, "Who Am I?"

The first and most important aspect to consider when asking who you are is to know *whose* you are. You, my dearest loves, are children of God, princesses created in His image and designed for greatness. You embody the beauty and grace He desires the rest of humanity to see and know. You are a display of all virtue and beauty. You have been meticulously crafted and patterned by the Master Weaver into a work of art designed to express God's love to all you see and know. You are beautifully and wonderfully made.

The second matter I want you to know is that *you are Daddy's most precious treasures.* You are loved, cared for, and cherished; you are the apple of my eye, my sunrise in the mornings, and stars shining ever so bright in the night sky. You are gifted, talented, admired. You are passionate, inquisitive, and unstoppable. You are loved. Your identity is not determined or predicated by external objects or empty philosophical ideologies.

External voices will always draw your attention to the vein and superficial aspect of what others consider to be your identity, beauty, and self-worth – always changing, always wanting, always empty, and eager to subtlety persuade that you have no intrinsic worth and who and whose you are. In this, your identity can be bartered for a life of depression, loneliness, self-loathing, depravity, and emptiness. All the negativity masquerades as contentment, all the while filtering away your happiness.

I have met too many young girls and women who have personally shared their heartbroken stories about how they've sought to know who they are through lifestyles that left them void, empty, and hurting. By the time they arrived on my doorstep, they'd been in such a predicament. They'd yielded themselves to anything and anyone who came along to satisfy their temporal need for meaning and identity. They were motivated by a desire to be known and belong. That way of living is disturbing and destructive. The philosophy of trying everything has left many women in a desert of loneliness and misery, losing their identity and meaning, longing to find who they are and whose they become an unattainable reality relegating their lives to live in constant pursuit and wanting.

Who you are is not found in the likes and views on a social media page; it can't be found through the pages of a magazine or television screen, nor in music videos or cinema. It can't be found in a friendship or relationship with a man. You must protect and deliver yourself against all of life's entrapments and pursue the greatest gift bestowed upon you, *love*. With that one word, it is meant to encompass your love for God, love for your family, and love for yourself.

As you grow older, you will begin to see through many of the external forces. Those forces try to lure you in by creating doubt in who you are and compel you to abandon all reasons to live with positive characteristics such as honor, integrity, love, peace, humility, character, and commitment. You are born gold, don't let external forces turn your heart cold.

Remember your identity and *whose* you are. God loves you beyond measure, I love you to infinity, you are loved. Who am I? I am a child of God. Daddy's girls. You are my loves.

Remember,
Daddy loves you

My prayer

Dearest Lord, as with every aspect of life, trends and fabs will try to persuade my girls to lose their identity, I pray Your constant presence over their lives. I ask that you keep them through the many temptations and voices that will constantly question who and whose they are. I pray your hand of blessing and protection over their thoughts, hearts and lives. Amen.

Life

"Nor I-nor anyone else, can travel that road for you. You must travel it yourself."

WALT WHITMAN

My dearest Peanut and Chiqui,

I think of those moments and years when life was simple but full of love and laughter. How I long to hear you laugh uncontrollably to the point of tears. Thank you, my loves. You've brought much-needed joy to my life.

I take great pleasure in sharing this letter with you and expressing what the purpose and meaning of life are, according to my collective experiences and exchanges with life itself. The most important aspect in understanding what life all is about, is to know that life – first and foremost – is a beautiful gift. That's right. *Life is a gift.* Every day you wake up and have breath in your lungs, know that the day has been given to you as a gift by our beloved Creator.

I remember when we celebrated your birthdays or Christmas and you girls would be so excited and eager to open your gifts. You'd beg your mother and me to open them early because you were both gleefully expecting something wonderful and amazing. We took pictures to save the memories of your joy and expressions upon opening your presents. *Priceless.* In that same way, see each day as a gift you're eager and excited to open. Welcome the day with exuberance and enjoy. Live each day with an attitude of expectation, awe and wonder and you will see how the revelation of this wonderful truth will bring joy and peace to you and to all those around you.

Life is about accepting the unexpected. In your younger years, I remember sitting at the table and showing you a map of my journey through life. Your eyes grew wide when you saw how much I have traveled. Next to my map, I drew a map of your lives, and they were very short in comparison. I illustrated the roads, valleys and mountains I've traversed. Those journeys gave me the ability to see and understand that life is generous and abundant with unexpected events that alter your life and impact your human spirit.

Keep your eyes open. You must develop a keen ability to see that both good and bad unexpected events are part of the human experience. They are both designed for a specific goal and purpose; they are designed to teach you and bring you out of your comfort zone, make you grow and develop an appreciation for the things that matter most.

I was having dinner with a good friend whose husband had passed away. She shared with me that losing the love of her life, the person she most admired and who was her source of comfort and strength was the most painful experience she's yet had to live with. The hurt, pain, anger, regret, loneliness, and crushed spirit was difficult to bear. She expressed to me that she would take back all the *bad* moments in their marriage and exchanged them to have him again. She continued to share that the arguments and disagreements they'd had now seemed so insignificant and failed in comparison to having him alive. As her eyes watered and tears came down her cheeks, the voice of regret uttered, "I wish I would have not worked as much. I wish I would have done more. I wish..."

Here is my advice to you concerning life. Wake up every day as early as possible, start each morning in prayer and gratitude. Say and name what and who you are grateful for, welcome each day as a gift from God, and plan each day to do something special for someone else. Develop the discipline to journal your daily experiences and pour all your day's emotions and hardships into recording your day. Later you can see how far you've come. Enjoy the company you choose to surround yourself with, cherish the small moments that may seem trivial but are actually blessings in disguise. Forgive as often as possible, love with every fiber of your being, laugh till your stomach hurts, sing loud and bold, cry as much as you need to, and make sure you don't live in this world as a taker, but instead, live in this world as a giver.

Leave your impression, your mark so others can see how through all of life's hardships you were able to rise above and overcome. Share your gifts and talents with the world, share your art and song for all to see and hear. Remember that just as the lotus flower grows and blossoms in mud, so should your life grow and blossom in this world that is full of mud. Love God with all your heart, seek His wisdom and character and He will never leave your side.

Forever, my loves.

Remember,
Daddy loves you.

My prayer

Our heavenly Father, you are the author of life, and you are not limited by time or space. You know our every thought and breath. You knew my girls before they were ever thought of and every second of their existence. I pray you watch and order their steps. That as they live life, they may never forget You and Your Word. May they acknowledge and trust You in all their ways. I pray Your infinite blessings over my precious girls. Amen.

Love

"God is Love. Whoever lives in love lives
in God and God in them."

1 JOHN 4:16 NIV

My dearest Peanut and Chiqui,

My deepest desire is to ensure you know how much I love you. To kiss and hold you in my arms once more and breathe in your sweet scent. Oh, how I love you, my girls. This letter is difficult to write because, in my opinion, it's about the highest of all virtues, this letter is about love and its power to change your life and heart. Unfortunately, the word *love* has lost its truest meaning. People today use it to express it to their favorite soft drinks, televisions shows, sports, art, media, and every other emotional attachment that can be conjured. Although emotions do express an aspect of love, it's more than that. The dictionary defines love as "a great interest or pleasure in something or to feel deep affection for someone." Notice how emotions and pleasure are descriptors of love.

For me, love is more than an emotion, mood, feeling, or pleasure. Love is a principle which regardless of emotion, feeling, or mood, loves and gives unconditionally. Many people view love as conditional. It's conditional because of what it gets in return. For as long as people get what they want and feel happy with the object or person at hand, the world is a beautiful place.

But what about when you love someone so deep in your heart and it's not reciprocated? What about when someone is unfaithful and breaks your heart? What if someone destroys your name and reputation? What about when the person closest to you lies and betrays your trust? I can go on. The truth is that love keeps no record of wrongdoing. Love forgives, love is not selfish or unkind, it does not envy and endures all things. I know that's hard to hear, but it's true.

These virtues are difficult to understand because in the culture and time we live in, love has been reduced to the lowest of all forms-an emotion, which no essence of truth can ever be built on.

As your father, the love I have for you is deep and profound. I think and dream of you always, I smile, and my heart skips a beat when I hear your voice. The way I speak and treat you are expressions of my love, the way I serve you and pray for you every night is of my deepest affection. And although I know you will make mistakes along the way and may go the wrong course and make decisions that may break my heart, I will never stop loving you. You will forever be my Peanut and Chiqui. From the day you were born to the time you read this letter and beyond, I hope and pray I have modeled for you, shown you, told you how much I love you and how much I have loved the love of my life, my queen, your beautiful mother.

So let me tell you a little bit about your mother. In the many years we've been together, your mommy has been through every storm with me. We've had wonderful joyous times and we've experienced sorrow, hurt, betrayal, and pain. We have suffered great setbacks and experienced incredible victories. And through it all, your mother has always expressed, lived, and showed how much she loves me. Despite all my imperfections and times when I've been very difficult, your mother never stopped loving me and believing in me. And the love we both have for you girls goes beyond what you will ever know or imagine.

Some of life's toughest lessons will require you to show your truest love to someone or something, especially, when they don't deserve it. That's right, even when they don't deserve it. I would be remiss if I didn't mention that there will be times when your heart will be broken, shattered, and torn into pieces, you will cry many tears and experience the worst of pain and sorrow a person can ever feel. But despite all those things, I will tell you with all confidence and assurance, love never fails, it always wins.

And when you love someone and that person loves you back unconditionally, then that love becomes the greatest of all joys and truest pleasure.

Love is a principle, not an emotion. Love is the greatest of all virtues. Love is perfection. God is love.

Remember,

Daddy loves you!

My prayer

Dear Lord, I pray your grace and mercy over my girls. I pray that they may come to experience Your love, compassion, and kindness in such ways that they will grow confident in their relationship with You. May Your love abound much in their lives and may they never seek to find it elsewhere or replace Your love with a poor imitation. I bless my girls with all of heaven's love. Amen.

Forgiveness

"...But as I got closer to the car that would take me away, I realized that when I went through the gate, if I still hated them, they would still have me. I wanted to be free. And so, I let it go."

NELSON MANDELA

My dearest Peanut and Chiqui,

I think of you often and wish to be by your side. I yearn to hear about your day and what made you smile. Oh, how I love you, my girls.

This next letter is extremely difficult to write because it deals with a very sensitive matter that many of us refuse to give our attention to and desire to avoid. *Forgiveness.*

Throughout my life, I have experienced so many wrongs. Some of these hurtful actions came from family, friends, acquaintances, colleagues, and strangers. Most of the wrongs and hurts came from family members and close intimate friends. For as long as I can remember, and as early of memories I have of my childhood, I have endured great hardships and abuse. For many years I compartmentalized much of the pain and sorrow, suppressing it and burying it deep in my heart and soul. My heart became ill-will and resentful and although I became a master at masquerading my pain and hurt, it was expressed in other ways toward people who I cared deeply for and who I knew loved me.

The truth is that many times, I would use the pain to push myself, I wanted to prove people wrong so much so that I elevated my education status to confirm that I was not broken but educated. The relationships I tried to develop and the life I attempted to create were on a value system that ignored the many wrongs done to me, which unfortunately led me to constant setbacks and resentments. The most interesting caveat in all of this was that I eventually discovered that much of the resentment, anger, and bitterness I felt was not toward others, but instead, toward myself. Eventually, I came to terms with my past and all its ailments and realized that I was living in a cell – a prison to which I sentenced myself. A prison where the four walls were bitterness, anger, resentment, and loneliness. The only difference between an actual prison and the one I manufactured and lived deep within was that my prison had no door. I had the freedom to walk out anytime I wanted or desired. Sadly enough, I chose to remain a willing prisoner of my past, holding myself in contempt.

The process and journey to forgiveness is not an easy one my love. Neither is one that should ever be pushed, pressed, ridiculed, or maligned by anyone if someone is not ready to take a long and painful walk to freedom. When I began my journey to forgiveness, I realized that it was going to take commitment, discipline, and a strong desire to live free. As I started the process, I traced back my earliest memory of wrongdoing.

I can clearly remember when I was three years old, looking on from the airport terminal, watching my mother boarding a plane to the United States, embarking on her own journey leaving me behind. I couldn't understand why my mother would do that. I felt rejected, abandoned, and exposed. Yes, exposed to predators and abusers; I had no sense of protection. My father refused to acknowledge my existence and refused to give me his last name until my grandmother got a hold of him and dragged him to the hospital so he could sign my birth certificate. I personally never met him. And so went my life, one hurtful experience after another. And as often as they came, I buried them deep inside. Rejection from my parents was perhaps one of the most painful and horrific experiences I've had to live with. I did not ask to come into this world to suffer, how can God allow for this to happen to me? More on God in another letter.

I am not going to recant all my painful experiences, but I wanted to give you an example of my first encounter with pain and forgiveness. Later, when I decided to walk out of my prison, I discovered this incredible truth, forgiveness became my spring well, my fountain of life. It yielded an abundance of joy and peace once I understood that forgiveness was not so much for the person who'd hurt me, but instead, forgiveness was for me.

My deepest and sincere wish is for you to live a life filled with love, peace, and joy. The reality is that life is not only about all those wonderful moments and seasons. Winter will come, seasons of pain and hardship will knock at your door, sorrow and regret will invite themselves and you will have to decide whether you will spend the rest of your life behaving despondent and morose – imprisoned by the four walls of bitterness, anger, resentment, and loneliness. My dearest loves, do not spend your life imprisoned by pain, or hold ill-will toward humanity. Trust me, you do not want to live there. I refused to live like a victim, instead, I chose to live free. I will be praying for you so when those moments come, you will have the strength and courage to forgive. I love you, my darlings.

Remember always,
Daddy loves you.

My prayer

Our heavenly Father, watch over my girls as they will inevitably have to go through some of life's greatest pain and sorrow.

Guide and comfort them as they will need to go through the process of forgiveness and be tempted to be imprisoned by their pain and aggressor. I ask You to remind them that in Christ and His death on the cross, He not only bore our pain and misery but forgave all our transgressors. It's the mystery and power of the cross. Strengthen their hearts, spirits, and souls, and may they live free to forgive, for forgiveness is a gift underserved. Amen.

Suffering

"If there is a meaning in life at all, then there must be a meaning in suffering. Suffering is an ineradicable part of life, even as fate and death. Without suffering and death human life cannot be complete."

VIKTOR E. FRANKL

My dearest Peanut and Chiqui,

I often reminisce of times we would be in the car or at home singing show tunes, commercials, jingles, Disney classics ending up laughing to no end. We had great moments together. I clearly remember all the joy and satisfaction I felt being with you. I sometimes think it went too fast; I wish you would have remained a child so we would have kept the laughter going. Such love I felt being around you.

This letter today will be about suffering. A very conflicting and undesirable topic to discuss, but necessary because it's part of life.

The Latin root of the word *passion* means to "suffer or endure." This word passion is used today to describe someone's strong desire or an activity they devote time and effort to, it's usually used to show a positive feeling or emotion toward a way of living or doing something. For example, you may have heard people say, "music is my passion." But what does that mean? Today, it usually translates to, *I really enjoy music*, and it ends there. But when you trace the origins of the word, its true meaning is quite different. It means to suffer and endure great pain or sorrow for the outcome of the desired. The best example I can give you is *The Passion of Christ*. More on this later. For as long as humans have been alive, the question always comes up, *Why do we have to suffer so much in this life?*

There are many reasons why people experience suffering. Some possible reasons why people suffer are perhaps due to, poor planning, an inability to make informed decisions, irrational thinking, emotional commitments, a lack of discipline, and self-control. These are all triggers that lead to unnecessary suffering. If people would take time to consider all the unintended consequences their choices have, they will experience less suffering. Suffering can also come in a different form, at times piercing our hearts and feeling it deep in our marrow. We usually experience it when we lose the love of our lives, or when a close family member dies.

When tragedy strikes unexpectedly, when we lose a job, or when we receive a diagnosis of cancer, a tragic death, or illness. We can also experience the horrors of suffering when parents lose a child, or when a person is a victim of rape and abuse. This type of suffering is quite difficult because we cannot find the answers within ourselves. We try to rationalize and think of probabilities or potential reasons why these unfortunate events happened, but to no avail. The worst part of these experiences is that, if we do not handle them correctly, it will lead us down a self-destructive path.

My dearest loves, suffering though a mystery, it's an inevitable part of life. It will come. Sooner or later, it will come and when it does, it's important to embrace it and accept it. Don't fight it, for the more you do, the deeper the wound, consequently delaying your growth. This is my advice to you.

As certain as seasons change, so will you. Throughout your life, you will experience the springs that will bud and blossom new ideas and opportunities for growth. Your summers will be full of sunshine, beach days, and relaxation. Your autumns will bring summer to an end and harvest time when you get to reap all you sowed ushering a wind of change preparing you for the winter ahead. Your winters are designed to prepare and restore you. Building, strengthening and conditioning your mind, body, spirit, and soul. It gets you ready for your next cycle.

Suffering in many ways can be compared to winter, but it's only when you understand the true value and purpose it has, that you will then see that suffering is essential and meaningful for life to have meaning. Suffering just for the sake of suffering is silly and foolish. It's only when we have a reason and a purpose for our suffering, that we will figure out its hidden blessings and treasures, which produce the sweetest of joys.

If in life, you happen to lose everything and find yourself through the darkest hours of your life, do not surrender the last of your freedoms, your ability to choose how you will think and respond. Do not surrender your will to fight, persevere, and purpose. When our suffering has a purpose, we find a *how*.

One last thing, suffering is a very painful experience. But you must remember that you never have to face it alone. The man of sorrows will walk with you. He knows all your pain and hurt. He promised to be by your side and never leave. He will give you strength and courage when you need it most, just don't forget to include Him in your healing process. He's always ready and willing. I love you, my angels.

Remember,

Daddy loves you.

My prayer

Our Father in heaven, suffering is painful and extremely unpleasant. However, I have learned that suffering is an essential and critical part of every person's life. It's in suffering that we find the true meaning of life and a reminder of what really matters, and the revelation of what things are worth. I pray that as my girls go through life, that they may see and find You in their suffering. May they know they have the free will to determine how they will respond to such egregious events that cut the heart and scar the soul. May Your precious hand lighten the sting of the pain and may Your gentle touch heal the brokenness in their spirit. May the man of sorrows, be their ever-present comforter. Please watch over my precious loves. Amen.

Humility

"Humility means having a proper perspective on ourselves, of seeing ourselves as we really are. It also means knowing that every person has equal worth."

MEG MEEKER, M.D.

My dearest Peanut and Chiqui,

As I write this letter, I feel like the happiest dad in the world for having such loving, kind, and caring daughters who fill my heart with joy and wonder. Oh, how I love you girls. As you read this letter, I want you to think about the word *humility.* This word is not very popular in our culture and in our time. As a matter of fact, I feel as if humility has been at odds with the human heart since forever. For many people, humility is a noble thought or perhaps a good goal to reach. It's an idea or desire but never manages to become a virtue worth pursuing.

Some people however can make this virtue of humility a life mission because they have understood the value and power humility has and its ability to provide for those who seek to live a more peaceful fulfilling life. Such was the exceptional life of Mother Teresa.

No one is born naturally humble or possessing humility. No one says, *Today I'm going to be humble and practice humility so people can see how great and amazing I am.* Like fear and faith, humility and pride cannot reside in the heart of man. It's either one or the other, never both.

Like riches and wealth, those who seek it, will become poor in virtue and bankrupt in principle if they don't have the right perspective of who they are in relation to others. Wealth and riches are a byproduct of dedication, discipline, commitment, hard work, and a diligent spirit. Those who find prosperity find it by committing their lives to a higher purpose, one of honor and respect. Who they become in the process is worth more than any amount of money.

Humility is not what you say as a mantra to yourself every morning, is not a wish or a strong idea for improving yourself. Humility comes with time and discipline. It comes when you understand who you are and not what you think you are. The secret is to begin examining your character closely, looking at your thoughts and behavior patterns. Also, acknowledge how you treat and speak to people. How much do you value your life or lifestyle over others? Understand your frailties and shortcomings and commit your life to one of servanthood. You must be assertive and confident in who you are and your purpose for living. You must have an unwavering discipline to learning and showing compassion to others, for when you take time to hear their stories you will understand why people are the way they are.

Humility is meeting a need that goes beyond your personal benefit. It comes when you truly value another person's life and honor them with great love and respect regardless of their background or how you're treated. Humility is not a weakness but a virtue that matures through pain and suffering. There are many who interpret humility as a way of living in poverty, lacking motivation and lack of desire to improve their social-economic status. For others, humility is a sign of weakness that should be avoided at all costs.

When considering if you choose to live a life of pride and arrogance, know that you will be digging an early grave for yourself. You will have given your life an early sentence to dying while destroying others along the way. Pride is so destructive; it destroys everything in its path. It shows no mercy and is always self-serving. Pride is the root of all things evil.

My dearest girls don't drink from that bitter fountain, its waters do not quench your thirst, instead, it pollutes and dehydrates your human heart.

I encourage you to read the lives of great men and women who through their pain and suffering discovered a new way of living. A new way of true power and strength, they found humility. The men and women we revere and honor have paid a price for what they strongly believed in and made it their life's mission to achieve that desire. It often means, letting go of pride and opening the door to meekness and humility.

As you begin this journey, you will have a lot of negative experiences that will try to harden your heart and convince you to think of yourself and your interest first. People who are filled with pride are usually takers; they don't invest in the world, nor do they contribute to it. A humble person will look at the condition and needs of the present world and say, *What can I give to the world?* True strength and power can only be found in meekness and humility. Love your neighbor, feed the hungry, clothe the naked, provide for the widow, care for the elderly, instruct the child, and care for your community. A life of humility is a life well-lived.

Remember,
Daddy loves you.

My prayer

Dear Father, I pray for Your character to be ever-present in the lives of my girls. I desire for the virtue of humility as displayed by Christ as He washed His disciples' feet and the rendering of His life as a ransom for our sins, be the same character found in my girls. May they see that a life worth living is a life that is of service, care, and love for others. May they have the correct view of themselves in relation to others as we all have been created in the image of God and endowed by our creator to live in dignity and respect for all human life. Amen.

Kindness

"All the beautiful sentiments in the world weigh less than a simple lovely action."

JAMES RUSSELL LOWELL

My dearest Peanut and Chiqui,

Oh, how I treasure your laughter and joy. Your ability to fill our home with such warmth and love brings peace and gratitude to my heart. This letter is on a topic that is very dear to me, and I desire to share it with you. I often think about what the world needs more of, and what can it benefit greatly from? And as I've pondered these questions, I'd like to shed some light on the matter. What I think our world needs more of is *kindness.* Although the word *kindness* sounds simple and an admirable thing to do, it's actually a very difficult feat to accomplish. Why? Why do I think there is very little kindness shown and given in our world? Why is it that we don't hear of it as often and see it as frequently? Yet when we do, we're inspired. Is the world really that bad?

The media markets and the external forces that control and dictate what you watch have one job, and that job is to design for viewers a mechanism where you are presented with an altered reality. A film that will focus on a particular paradigm and persuade you to view the world we live in as is presented – by those external forces.

Some examples of this altered reality are violence, depravity, deception, murder, hate, gossip, slander, abuse, fear, promiscuity, and more. The reason they present this as the reality of the world is that lewd or violent content sells. There is a market for this garbage where people pay billions of dollars to present a product that is so debased and destructive. These media markets are the recipients of great wealth, selling a product that speaks to the worse of human nature. And the sad truth is, people pay to watch it. Kindness to the external forces is not a lucrative investment.

Here's another thought. People, in general adults, are a by-product of their childhood and their collected experiences. Who they are and how they behave, think, and speak are the result of an environment. For many people, kindness is impossible to give because of what they experienced in the past; pain, anger, hatred, abuse, and failure. For others, there is no love, forgiveness, or gratitude in their hearts. Self-serving pride has a hold of them and when the heart has been broken and shattered so many times, it's difficult to show kindness. An unforgiven heart is unable to express genuine love and affection toward others. Kindness is a powerful virtue because is a byproduct of a grateful heart and a life that loves and forgives.

Here is my advice to you my princesses, as you will be challenged and confronted with moments and opportunities to display kindness to those who are undeserving. As noble and commendable it is to show kindness to those who are kind to you, it's of greater value and far more impacting to show kindness to those who hurt you.

Remember what I said to you before in other letters, people have a story. If you listen closely and pay attention, you will hear and see that they are displaying results from the people who hurt them. I'm not excusing their behavior, but by learning more about a person, you will gain a greater understanding of their shortcomings and devastating pain. Don't be quick to judge, God waits till the end of days to judge our lives.

Listen intently and compassionately, it matters and makes a difference. Don't grow tired of doing good and being kind to others, you will reap the great benefits of a life well-lived. Remember, to treat every person you meet with all the kindness you can muster. This will be the great secret to your success. While others conduct themselves in unbecoming behavior by gossiping, slandering, and humiliating others, you instead spend your life doing acts of kindness everywhere you go.

Value people and take time to hear their stories, you will be surprised at what you find deeply rooted in a person's heart – if you're willing to listen. Today is a great day to practice and show kindness to someone. Remember the question, *What does the world need more of?* The world needs more *you* and *your kindness.* The world will benefit from your choice to be kind, loving, patient, and gracious. Look past the obvious. See the person and understand their situation.

May kindness light your path and may you reap and enjoy the seeds you planted in the garden of life.

Remember,
Daddy loves you.

My prayer

Dearest Lord, it's my prayer that as my girls grow older, they will see the great virtue and blessing of living a life of kindness. The beauty and riches found in extending a hand in time of trouble, of giving a hug in time of sorrow, of rendering good to others, and living a life build on the principle and virtue of kindness, is one that makes your heart glad. May the fruits of the Spirit be the pillars by which they live and model the life of Christ to others. May your everlasting kindness never depart their side. Amen.

Purpose

"The man without a purpose is like a ship without a rudder- a waif, a nothing, a no man. Have a purpose in life, and, having it, throw such strength of mind and muscle into your work as God has given."

THOMAS CARLYLE

My dearest Peanut and Chiqui,

My heart longs to see you, my princesses. I think of you often and what you might be doing or what ideas are running through your minds. I miss you so much. The thought I want to share with you today is on the word *purpose.* In my opinion, this word *purpose* is one that gives direction and meaning to the journey through life. It will define your objective and goal in life. It will make you focus and intentional in everything you do.

The challenge many wonderful people face today and have always is that a purpose has not been defined or articulated where it becomes part of everyday life. If you ask people what their purpose in life is, many will say, *I don't know*, some might say, *To live a good life and be nice to everyone I meet*, while others may say, *To accomplish my dreams* – without offering any specificity. Few will tell and show you what their purpose is by the way they live.

As you read this letter my loves, take a few minutes to ponder the question, what is my purpose in life? The truth is that the question sounds simple, but it's difficult to answer because it forces you to look inwardly and evaluate your priorities, time, and commitments. It allows you to consider what you should value and should be doing, but instead, it exposes what you really think and do. This contrast of reality that lives within us, holds us back from ever accomplishing and living a life fulfilled by the purpose we have committed our lives to. A life with purpose is a life well-lived.

Unfortunately for me, this topic of *purpose* has been a lifelong struggle. I have concluded that purpose can be applied and found in many aspects or places in your life journey. You can have a purpose for education, arts, creativity, humanity, family, friends, career, justice, or finances. And then there is another type of purpose with a higher calling to generate long-term impact and meaning. That purpose will call you to live a life the world will remember long after you're gone. This life of *definitive purpose* will call you to the highest level of living, discipline, and passion. It will give no rest to your soul till you commit your hands to it, till you see it come to past. This is what we have been created for and given a few days in this life to make the most of it, to leave our mark, and leave the world better than we found it. The brevity of life is real, and time will never stop for anyone.

The *definitive purpose* is of the highest calling because it requires sacrifice, perseverance, grit, tenacity, and courage to overcome. All the external voices will tell you that your purpose is misplaced and that you should not pursue it because in the end you will be disappointed, or it will never come to fruition. Know that when you commit your life to a calling greater than yourself, you will suffer, pay a price and endure many setbacks. Don't look at them as discouragements, but instead use them, harness the negativity and pressure to let it fuel your life masterpiece. The things that have the most meaning and value in life require our greatest effort, time, energy, and focus.

Live with purpose, desire, and grit. No one is going to give you your purpose. Search for it, seek it, sort it and be intentional, zealous, ardent on living it out every day of your life. After all, there is no other way to live. A life without purpose is an idle life that loses meaning. Live with the *definitive purpose* to add value to others, to invest in your family, friends, and community. Live to help those in need, those who are sick, visit the elderly, care for the orphan and widow, live with the definitive purpose to show love and kindness, live to be all that He has beautifully crafted and designed you to be. Purposed to live purposely. I love you, my girls! Don't choose a life; live a life.

Remember,
Daddy loves you.

My Prayer

Our heavenly Father, before my girls were born, all of their living days were counted in your book of life and not one thought or action is omitted or overlooked. You have created them and allowed them to be born for this generation. For such a time as this. May they discover the true purpose of their existence, may they live out the God-given call to impact this present generation. May my precious girls unveil and see that the very essence and purpose of their lives is to be in communion with you. Guard their hearts and watch their steps as they will need your strength and courage to live out all they were created to do. Amen.

Self-Discipline

"The ability to make yourself do what you should do, when you should do it, whether you feel like it or not."

ELBERT HUBBARD

My dearest Peanut and Chiqui,

As I write this letter, I find my mind wandering and thinking about all the other things I think I should be doing and must eventually do. I realized that I give into these constant thoughts more frequently than I should. And if I do today, I will never be able to finish writing this letter to you.

You see, life in many ways is exactly like this, subtle. It's when you are going to work on something that is meaningful, something that brings you joy and fulfillment, the mind tends to wander and think of other things. The worst part of it all is that we have a tendency to give in to those distractions. When this happens, we've lost so much of our time, reversed our priorities, and given importance to something less deserving. What I want to share with you today is the beauty of discipline, its value, and its incredible benefit to your life.

I must confess that I have lived a good portion of my life undisciplined and given to distractions. And although I've been able to accomplish a lot in my life, I've realized that I've been able to do so because I was committed and focused on the outcome and the goal.

However, there are many areas in my life that I have not been so dedicated to. I've allowed distractions to prevent me from accomplishing dreams, goals, and desires, all because I placed too much value on trivial distractions. The word *discipline* has many meanings, for example, parents at times will discipline their children when they are misbehaving and in need of correction. Then, there is the discipline of work, profession, career; the work we do is our discipline, it's what we do for a living, it's the way we make money. And then there is the discipline of extreme focus, unwavering commitment to live a life filled with purpose and the intent to accomplish and reach a desired goal. This virtue is what has turned simple ordinary men and women into titans and virtuosos. These people understood the value of living a disciplined life, giving up temporal gratification for long-term satisfaction and wealth.

Some people choose to discipline their lives by watching what they eat. They want to have a healthy lifestyle. They exercise, get enough sleep, eat the right foods, and are constantly monitoring what they put in their bodies and mind. Others are disciplined with their money and are very selective on how and in what they spend it on. Others may focus on their talents and creative outputs. Creative people tend to be monomaniacal about their artistry and tend to protect their creative minds. They are constantly seeking and searching for beauty in nature and objects around them. The person who lives a disciplined life is not just able to accomplish more things in life, but live better lives.

The *secret sauce* to accomplishing any dream or desire is to be disciplined and committed to your craft and artistry. Do not negotiate this principle. Learn to embrace solitude as a necessity, not as a punishment. Solitude is the place where you reflect, meditate, pray and become more familiar with who you are, your weaknesses, and areas for growth. In this place of solitude, your ideas will take wings and your creativity finds a canvas to display your best work yet. See discipline as a way of life, never to be compromised or bartered.

A life plagued by distractions and vices is a life filled with failure, regret, and remorse. Always wanting and wishing to have written a book, composed a song, eaten healthy, gotten in shape, read more, saved money, invested, traveled, or prayed more. The list goes on.

My precious girls, the reason why so many people are not able to live great productive lives, is because they don't value the virtue of discipline and often give their time, mind, strength, and talent to meaningless distractions. You must, at all costs, protect yourself from this great evil. When all the motivation and good feelings disappear, the only thing that will keep you focused and moving forward is discipline. Discipline will not appear to be enjoyable at the moment, but it will bring great blessings, health, and peace to your soul.

My beautiful princesses, you are extremely talented and gifted. Continue to work on your art, music, education, prayer life. Value your time. Don't squander it by doing things that take you away from your dreams and heart's desire. Discipline yourselves to live a life well-lived.

Remember,
Daddy loves you!

My prayer,

Dear Lord, I pray my girls will have the grit and ability to develop self-discipline in their craft, work, and life. May they discover the wonder and beauty, and blessings self-discipline can be and the impact it will generate in their personal life and their family. Nothing worth pursuing can ever be accomplished or obtained without a strong desire and discipline, may their heart and daily walk be in constant pursuit and desire for you, Lord. Please bless my girls. Amen.

Time

"Do not wait; the time will never be 'just right.' Start where you stand, and work with whatever tools you may have at your command, and better tools will be found as you go along."

NAPOLEON HILL

My dearest Peanut and Chiqui,

I often ask myself the question, *Where did the time go?* How come life seems to move at a pace I can't control or stop? This thought is not unique nor is uncommon for many people. We use such expressions to convey a feeling that life is slipping through our fingers, fleeting, while we fear the inevitable. We worry that we have not made much of what we're supposed to with the time allotted to live a great life.

I do wish, however, that I would have discovered earlier in my life how valuable and essential time really is and to make good use of it. But like a mentioned before, we cannot live a life of regret, constantly thinking of the past and the memories of lost time for which we will never get back. We don't get do to it over. In essence that's the beauty of life, you must live in the moment making every second of your life count.

Most people don't realize how precious time is and the impact it has on a person's life. When you begin to understand and look closely at what you give your time to, then you will realize who you are and what you value most. Your mouth may say something else, but your time shows who you really are. Time is your greatest asset, do not squander it, you only have but a limited supply, choose wisely who or on what you will invest it on. If you are going to write a book, focus on that and make it part of your day, write it in your calendar, and don't compromise that time.

If you are working on your art, prepare and organize a space that will inspire you constantly and motivate you to stay focused. When practicing your instrument and music, set a time to increase and improve your ability and craft. Don't leave it for tomorrow – you don't live in tomorrow, you live in the present. Many things can happen if you leave it for later. If you spend time with close friends, don't think about anything or anyone else but be in the moment, let them know they matter, give them your undivided attention.

Make certain things a priority in your life such as family, close friends, travel, your talents, God, prayer, reading, solitude, exercising, laughing, and dancing. Don't give your time to things that will not add value to your life and to those around you. Protect your time from the trivial things of life, such as too much television, social media, distractions, or too much sleep. These time stealers will make you poor and steal your very breath of life. You will find it difficult later in life to loosen their grip on you and your time.

One of the most valuable pieces of advice I can give you is, *make time for God every day.* This should be non-negotiable. Take an hour a day to spend in prayer and reading the Bible. This is critical to your success and your life. Do not compromise this time for when you go through difficult moments, God will be the only one who will give you hope, wisdom, and strengthen your heart.

See time as an investment, the more you invest your time in meaningful works, the more successful and fulfill you will be. Protect your time by saying no to things that are designed and intended to stop your progress and purpose. Fight off the darts of laziness, apathy, and procrastination. The only way to live is with intent and a clear vision for *time.*

My dearest girls, when you get older and you look back on your life, you will ask yourself one question, did I make the most out of life? Did I have time for adventure? Did I make time for my family? Did I invest my time well? Stay focused and make today count. Remember, we don't get to do things over, be intentional on how you use your most valuable asset, time.

As I write this letter, I look back to when you girls were born, and how I held you in my arms, kissed you, and couldn't stop smelling your fresh baby scent. I wanted to spend every waking moment with you. When I see you now, I see that you are getting older, wiser, more beautiful, and gracious. I do wish at times you both would have remained little girls, but then I realized, that time stops for no one. Therefore, I want every moment I spend with you to count. To matter. To mean everything. I love you so much, my beautiful girls.

Remember,
Daddy loves you!

My prayer

Heavenly Father, I pray with each passing day, my girls learn more about the value of time and how when used wisely, time becomes a great asset and blessing. To honor each day of life and take advantage of the many opportunities a day brings. The gift of having twenty-four hours in a day is afforded to everyone and it's what we do within those hours that matter most and determines how fulfilled we will live. May they use time wisely to seek and honor You. Amen.

Distractions

"Spring has passed. Summer has gone. Winter is here...and the song that I meant to sing remains unsung. For I have spent my days stringing and unstringing my instrument."

RABINDRANATH TAGORE

My dearest Peanut and Chiqui,

It seems appropriate to write to you, my beautiful girls about distractions as it's one of those subtle things that can destroy your dreams. Quite often we dream, aspire, and make plans on how to achieve and accomplish all that we want to be. We have dreams of becoming great artists or rock stars, famous, successful, and wealthy. And although there is nothing wrong with those desires, it's important to understand that the very things we wish for and dream of will never happen unless there is a plan, commitment, and discipline. How you live your life and the things you give your time and effort to will determine your level of success and accomplishment.

As I have gotten older and more observant, I realized that distractions have been by far the most detrimental and destructive part of my life. It has come in many forms and it's important to identify them and discipline your life to overcome and get rid of them as much as possible. The one aspect of distraction is that distraction is your greatest enemy. It comes disguised in pleasure and appealing objects, but its intent is to hinder destroy and forbid you from accomplishing your goal, leaving the sting of regret and guilt. Distraction is a deadly disease, one that must be eradicated ferociously without mercy or pity.

Distractions will come when you are working on a beautiful masterpiece, when you are writing your best novel yet or when you are designing and creating gorgeous artwork. Distraction will come when you are trying to do something meaningful and add value to your life. Distraction will come in the form of friends, family, television, and media. It will come in the form of hunger, thirst, tiredness, fatigue, restlessness, and discouragement. It will gradually and very subtle usurp all of your attention by imagining that you have to get chores and errands done, you will begin to feel like suddenly there are so many things to get of your schedule. Then you will realize that the one thing you needed to do, was ignored, forgotten, or put to the side for the next day, only to repeat the same regrettable pattern of giving into distractions.

Learn to say no to a lot of things so you can focus on what's important and a priority. You must try to keep a calendar to help you stay on target and finish what you set your heart to do. Develop a daily schedule where every minute is accounted for, yes, every minute is accounted for. Wake up, brush your teeth, make your bed, pray, read, meditate, and plan your day before you begin. Have breakfast and then begin to do your best work. Take time to exercise, go for walks, eat a healthy meal, and rejuvenate yourself with quality audio books, a podcast, or reading a book. It will help you in your journey to accomplishing your greatest dream yet.

Nothing will be given to you. You will need to work hard, be dedicated, committed, and disciplined if you want to succeed. How many hours will it take to master a piece of music? How many strokes of a paint brush will it take to paint the most desirable artwork? Do not blame anyone for where you are in your life. There are no viable or justifiable alibis to excuse yourself for not being your best. Leave excuses for those who only dream but who have no discipline or grit to work and see their dream become a reality.

You, my sweetest girls, have greatness in you. You have been gifted and blessed with such ability that I believe you are meant to leave your imprint in the world. As you journey throughout this life, you will be required to make a priority of spending time with God in prayer and reading His Word. Do not neglect that, it's the only discipline that will never disappoint or leave you wanting. Remember, distraction is subtle and evil, you must see it as such.

Don't ignore and never understatement its power. Before you know it, nothing you set your heart to do will be done. Kick distraction to the curve. Your dreams are worth your time. I love you my dearest girls.

Remember,
Daddy loves you.

My prayer

Dear Lord, I bless my girls for all you have created them to be. Throughout life, they will have many distractions to deter them from their dreams, goals, purposes, and commitments. Help them to see the importance of recognizing distractions and doing something about it. Let them build the courage to fight off things that are meant to prevent them from reaching their purpose and goal. Watch over them and keep them forever more. In Your care, I entrust my girls. Amen.

Debt

"The rich rule over the poor, and the borrower is slave to the lender."

PROVERB 22:7 NIV

My dearest Peanut and Chiqui

Perhaps nothing in life is more important than the peace of being debt-free and taking responsibility for your finances. This is by far one of the most important principles in life – the understanding of money – and how to be a good steward of it. Much of our society and economy functions and financial institutions rely on the consumption of goods and resources. The health of the economy is determined by how much people buy and borrow. This system in many ways has allowed for many to own things which if they had to save money, they would have waited a long time to purchase anything substantial. Although the ability to use credit and borrow money to purchase something you want immediately seems alluring and desirable, the unfortunate impact is, the more you borrow the less you own and the less you own the more you pay.

Borrowing or accruing debt in its simplest definition is owing money to someone or something for the purchasing of a product. Do not borrow money under any circumstances. Avoid at all costs. The facts are that millions of Americans live in a constant struggle to pay large amounts of debt they have accrued over a period of time. They have auto debt, credit card debt, and mortgage debt, home equity debt, student loan debt, vacation debt, and personal loan debt.

The most recent data shows that the total American debt is near 15 trillion dollars. This is extremely concerning because it shows where people put their confidence and how they handle their money. If a person earns one hundred dollars and uses 90% of it to pay debts, how will they save and live on 10% of their earnings? This is no way to live or behave as a good steward of money.

My darlings, my personal struggle with debt is very serious and sad, and that's why I want to share the true cost and impact living in debt has had on me and our family. Growing up, my mother had very little knowledge of finance but did the best she could to provide for her three sons. I didn't have a father growing up. The only men who passed through my life were dysfunctional and irresponsible, so they did not know how to balance income with expenses, much less building savings. I had no one to teach me or mentor me in many areas of life, particularly in the area of finances. It left many gaps in my fiscal education, leaving me exposed, vulnerable, and susceptible to making financial mistakes. This brought upon me a great deal of naiveness and ignorance when it came to handling money and being financially responsible.

When I started working, I realized that I could pay for things I wanted. I could make car payments and credit card payments and I was fine with it. Soon after, I found myself treading water in large amounts of debt. The money I earned suddenly seemed to have shrunk now that I had payments to make. My income was quickly consumed by paying off debt. This way of thinking carried over into my marriage, and it had an enormous impact on our lives. I did not save or invest money, I did not purchase any real estate, instead, I borrowed and paid for a very long time.

This lesson on debt and being financially responsible is critical that you understand and apply to your life. It will spare you from future grief and pain.

As you grow older and the possibility and desire for buying things become a reality, resist the temptation to borrow and go into debt. Trust me, my princesses, you will regret it and it will hold you back from living a peaceful and rich life. Do not buy things that lose value over time, such as, cars, clothes, home furniture, televisions, or any material thing that will depreciate in value. Save your money, invest your money, and own things that increase in value over time. Do not make a financial agreement with people who are irresponsible with their money; never co-sign or give your credit to anyone, especially family and friends. In the end, you will lose both, the family member and the money.

Remember, you are only but a steward of the money you earn, the money you make belongs to God because He gave you health, a mind, and an ability to make a living. Make good on the money He has entrusted in your care and know that God will bless you more when you are responsible with what you have been given. I mentioned before that I did not have a father growing up to teach, mentor and guide me in life, however, I would be remiss if I did not mention, that I am responsible for the poor financial decisions I made. I will not blame others for where I am in life. I take full responsibility for all the mistakes I've made. I have learned a lot and have gained wisdom and insight that I wish to share with you. Do not be a slave to the lender, instead, become so financially independent and you will see that your sleep will be sweeter and your days brighter. Live debt-free, there is no other way to live. I love you, my dear girls.

Remember,
Daddy loves you.

My prayer

Dearest Father, throughout my life I have seen the damaging impact debt has had on so many lives, including my own. You abhor debt and it's the reason why Your Word is clear that we should free ourselves from it quickly. I pray for wisdom, self-control, and discipline for my girls with their finances. I pray they attend to the money principles we've spoken of numerous times at home and understand the true value of being debt-free. I pray they do not become slaves to the lender. I pray complete financial freedom over my girls. Amen.

SEX

"But at the beginning of creation God made them male and female. For this reason, a man will leave his father and mother and be united to his wife, and the two shall become one flesh. So, they are no longer two, but one flesh. Therefore, what God has joined together, let no one separate."

MARK 10:6-9 NKJ

My dearest Peanut and Chiqui.

This perhaps may be the letter I anticipated writing to give my perspective to you both. For many generations sex has been treated as a taboo, a topic many parents have tried to avoid talking about, and perhaps for good reasons. It is uncomfortable to talk to our children, particularly our daughters about sex, what it means, its purpose, its power, responsibility, its pleasure, and its destructive consequences – if not properly handled.

Let me start by saying that the images presented in movies are flawed and misleading. They hold a philosophy that is also shared in schools, television shows, media, and by influential people. It is that they promote the idea that sex is something you should give yourself because you have a right to happiness and pleasure. Plainly speaking, it is irresponsible to think that you should try everything that comes your way and every person until you find what you like. Unfortunately, you will never be satisfied with anyone because the more you try, the more you lose all conscience of yourself, reality, value, and self-worth. This philosophical perspective of sex is cheap, worthless, and depraved.

The culture and times we live in are saturated with sex. The pervading intent of non-Christian society is always to rob children of their innocence. This is accomplished through visually stimulating young viewers to overly-sexualized images which will desensitize them from the harmful effects of immorality before they are mature or ready to handle it with responsibility. Sexual images appear everywhere, so much so that kids cannot view most streaming apps, social media platforms, magazines, television shows, movies, or even public transportation advertisements without being exposed to images of an overtly sexual nature. They aren't ready to handle the attraction of scantily dressed men or women, thereby piquing their curiosity prematurely without any regard for their innocence or emotional impact.

I know of women who have slept with many men. They've shared stories of how men have made them feel once they are done having sex. The following are some of their words. "I feel worthless after sleeping with another man," or "I feel used," I feel like I lost a piece of myself," or "I feel worthless and unloved." Others say, "I feel unwanted," I feel forgotten," and "I feel robbed."

Although in the moment of having sex they may feel pleasure, in the end, they feel remorse, regret, and self-loathing. Many women think that if they sleep with a man, that will keep him interested and motivate him to stay. Instead, many men see this as an act that women do with all men they date or like. Men, for the most part, are very insecure when it comes to sex. They often compare themselves to other men's tales and if a man sleeps with a woman, they assume many others already have or will. The unfortunate consequences of this are that some of these women start having sex from a very young age, some as young as twelve years old.

They start by being pressured by their boyfriend to masturbate, have oral sex, or anal sex. All these sexual acts lead many girls to live very promiscuous lives leaving them to face the dire consequences of their early sexual activities such as, STDs, HPV which leads to cancer, or unplanned pregnancies, leaving many women to deal with the aftermath of pregnancy, anxiety, depression, anger, or suicidal tendencies.

As mentioned earlier, I grew up without a father, and the men I had in my life were completely and utterly dysfunctional. I had one particular uncle who had an influence during my childhood. He taught me to objectify women and treat them as sexual objects. I kept this mindset throughout my teens, seeing girls as mere sexual objects without a care for their well-being or the impact a sexual relationship will have on them and their lives.

I held this view of women till I met your mother. I remember in many ways trying to convince and seduce her to have sex before marriage, but she never budged. "No! Not till we get married," she firmly stated. I had finally found a woman who knew her worth and value and was unwilling to comprise her virtue and trade it for a moment of pleasure to a lifetime of love and true intimacy. I chose your mother, not only because she is beautiful, but because she was worth waiting for, she knew her true value. The life we live and your existences are solely credited to your mother and her decision to say no, even under pressure, and wait till marriage to discover what God truly intended for a married couple to enjoy, a healthy sex life.

You see my girls, sex is a beautiful experience. Sex is a gift from God. He designed it not just to procreate but for your enjoyment as well. Sex within the scope of marriage is beautiful and its essence is discovered when it's mutually shared with the person you love and who loves you. Do not give yourself to men for instant gratification, it will leave you empty and void. It will never bring to you the happiness you may wish for, instead, it will reduce your self-worth and value leaving you empty and void. You are more than just a beautiful face and more than a body. Do not let the world objectify you; you are intelligent, talented, gifted, and of great worth.

You are worth waiting for, do not settle for anything less than your true value. Sex is divine and it's a gift from God. I love you so much!

Remember,
Daddy loves you.

My prayer

Dear Father, you created sex for procreation, our enjoyment, and for our pleasure; sex is sacred in your eyes. The mystery lies in how two become one and at conception three become one. You designed sex in perfection and is holy before your eyes. May my daughters see the beauty and joy in intimacy the way you designed it, may they remember their value and know they are worth waiting for. They are worth respect and admiration. May they wait till their marriage night to experience the beauty and great joy of a honeymoon. Keep them as they will be tempted, pressured, and ridiculed for what they believe. May your angels encamped around them and protect them from the evil one who plans to destroy their future. This is a father's prayer, a father's plea, to watch over my precious girls as they navigated a secular worldview on sex and how that system ob-

jectifies and strips women of their true value, worth, dignity, and identity. A father's heart prays. Amen.

Stages of Life

"Live a great life where you are, and in the daily work you have to do, and greater works will surely find you out. Big things will come to you, asking to be done."

WALLACE D. WATTLES

My dearest Peanut and Chiqui,

I clearly remember the day you were each born. I can recall seeing your tiny fingers, toes, and silky-smooth skin and how your baby skin felt pressed to my cheek. As you took your first breaths and cried – and made such a ruckus – my heart leaped for joy in awe and wonder of your beauty and tenderness. Witnessing your births was by far the greatest blessing and experience of my life. It was as if God smiled at me knowing I needed more beauty in my life. As your daddy, I always wished you would have stayed tiny, little, innocent, and dependent on me. I didn't mind changing your diaper, feeding you, holding you in my arms till you fell asleep. I would lay you on my chest and feel your tiny heartbeats next to mine; three hearts beating as one. Oh, how I loved every minute and second of watching you grow from babies to toddlers. I'm glad I was there to see it all.

The reality of life is that we all must grow – nothing ever stays the same; it's not meant to. As a father, I've had to realize that you will get older, and you will blossom and grow. I guess the question I would ask myself is, *Why am I reluctant for my baby girls to grow older? What am I afraid of?* Well, as a dad I've always been afraid of a few things. For starters, seeing you grow from babies to young girls, to teenagers, and eventually, adults always made me nervous because I would not be able to always shield you from the painful reality life can bring.

At times, life is brutal and disheartening, it has a way of piercing the depths of our hearts and stealing the very essence of joy and the purest of all pleasure, serenity. You must go through disappointment, heartbreak, sorrow, loneliness, and eventually defeat. I would not be a good dad if I didn't share with you the hardships that you will find on the road of life. It's part of the human experience.

The second aspect is that at some point, I must take off the training wheels and let you ride on your own. Nothing makes me more nervous than the thought of letting you go on your own. You will make decisions on the friends you wish to have, the man you will eventually marry, the clothes you want to wear, the music you will listen to, the job you want to have, the places you want to travel and the life you want to live. This is difficult just thinking about it because, just the other day, you were but just a baby.

I've tried my very best to be the dad I could be. I know I've made mistakes along the way, and I blundered some aspects of fatherhood, but know that you have always been top priority in my life. I'm merely but a steward of your life. God has given me charge to love you, to care for you in all moments of life, to teach the ways of our heavenly father, to model a life of character and integrity, to cherish and love and honor your mother, to prepare you for what's to come and to protect you at all costs. To listen to all your questions, concerns and to give you my undivided attention. These are some of the things I have tried to do to prepare you for life's greatest obstacles.

Here is my advice to you. Live your life with great expectation and excitement. Go on adventures and make wonderful memories, travel the road where no one else has, and make your own mark in this life. Don't ever live like a victim, blaming others for where you are in life, work hard, leave trails of beauty along the path of life. Make every moment count, be in the now, laugh till you cry, cry till you laugh, be fearless, courageous especially when discouragement creeps in. Make mistakes and learn from them. Love with all your heart and forgive with all your soul. Do not let anger or pain settle in your heart. Instead, protect your heart, love your friends, and people with their flaws.

The early stages of your life are necessary and keen to your success in adulthood. You will face many challenges and setbacks due to the strong pull from external forces that compel and seduce you to give in to all sorts of pleasures. Live with your eyes wide open, think long term, and the benefits of your choices. This principle applies to education, finances, and relationships... do not squander time, it's your most valuable asset.

As I now look back over your lives and how you have both blossomed into beautiful girls, I now understand that if I would have had it my way, I would have missed so many moments that have taken my breath away. I would have missed seeing you take your first step, watching your first two baby teeth come out, the very first time you utter the words *Da-da,* or when you finally said, "I love you, daddy."

I would have also missed you learning to ride your bikes, your first day of school, your first concert, your first birthday, your first day at the beach, and our first Christmas together. I also remember holding you so tight and comforting you when you both were getting stitches. As the surgeon began to mend your wound, you both said, "No more daddy no more!" It broke my heart seeing you go through so much pain, knowing the doctors would add more stitches and I couldn't spare you from the pain. The only thing I was able to do was to hold you, look you in the eyes, and reassure you that I was there with you and that I would never leave your side to experience such pain alone.

So now I understand that the next stages of your lives will be messy, painful, but necessary for a great life. I'm looking forward to seeing you grow and become the great CEOs, entrepreneurs, businesswomen, moguls, creators, innovators, titans of industry, artists, wives, daughters, mothers, and strong confident women you are destined to be.

There's one last thing I want to share with you and that is, the most important relationship you will need to develop, is your relationship with your heavenly Father. I am your earthly father and I hope I have been obedient to what my heavenly Father has asked of me. You will need to nurture and cultivate that relationship.

God knows your every breath, every moment, and every second of your life before you were both born. There are no secrets with God. He knows your every thought, idea, and emotion. He loves you and is for you, He will never let you down. He has blessed you with many wonderful gifts. Seek Him through His Word, He speaks every day, He is never silent. He is a much better father than I could ever be. He loves you and walks with you in and through every moment of your lives. You will forever be my Peanut and Chiqui.

Remember,
Daddy loves you.

My prayer

Dearest heavenly Father, life is short and brief. You did not create us so You can live in fear watching over us. You are all-knowing and all-powerful and are not limited or threatened by our opinions or views of who You are. You are perfect in all your ways. You live in eternity and our temporary residence here on earth is just that, temporary.

I pray that as my girls make their way through life, they may learn to appreciate every stage and season. Nothing ever remains the same. Show them the value of yesterday and of to-day. Although tomorrow is not promised to anyone, may they welcome it as a sign for growth and an opportunity to draw closer to you. Watch over them and cover them with your love. Amen.

Education

"The great aim of education is not knowledge, but action."

HERBERT SPENCER

My dearest Peanut and Chiqui,

One of the most important tools you will need to be successful in life is education. I use the word *tool* to describe education as a means to achieve a goal and develop our ability to understand and live within the perimeters of learning. Millions of people throughout the centuries have had the privilege and opportunity to learn and grow in their thinking to accomplish a desired goal or to achieve success. The traditional view of receiving or attaining education is through the method of schooling.

Children begin now as early as three years of age entering the big world of academia where their first experience in formal education is through the lens of social play, creating, developing motor skills, and stimulating their imaginations. This process continues as the child grows and is promoted grade by grade completing elementary school, middle school and high school, and sometimes college.

Though this system for learning and education is the standard for all children across the globe, there's something to be said, as to why students who obtain the same – or similar level – of education, some will succeed while others don't. Every child and person who attends schooling has been afforded the opportunity to learn, though we all learn differently and process information at different rates and through multiple lenses, it's critical to see and learn one key principle – how to use the knowledge you acquire and put it into action. The application of knowledge becomes essential, not merely gathering information for storing it into your long-term memory bank.

Education is not necessarily about going to college and learning everything there is to know about a particular matter or subject and, once you're done, you move on with your life. Education is a life pursuit. It's imperative to make learning the lynchpin, anchor, and pillar of your life. Never stop learning, reading, and being inspired by great men and women who have not just traversed this life but who have instead conquered, lived it, and left their imprints in the world. Learn from the best. As you grow older and your priorities evolve, develop the habit of reading as much as possible. Read at least two hours a day. This is non-negotiable. Learn about different topics and genres such as but not limited to, religions, cultures, biographies, history, the arts, sciences, business, investing, real estate, medicine, world leaders, and anything that will add value to your life and develop your ability to increase your worth and contribution to this world.

Learn from conversations you have with people. Take a person out for a cup of coffee or a latte and ask them to tell you their story. Ask questions such as, *What has been your greatest accomplishment, and why? What has been your biggest temporary defeat, why? What did you learn from those experiences?* These simple questions will open a world of knowledge and increase your level of education because now you have additional information to help you in your life's journey. Make travel part of your education. Save money to see the world and learn how people from different walks of life live.

Draw no judgment of others but look closely and intently to their way of thinking and philosophy of life. Be a student of life and of the world. When you're having a conversation with people who share a different perspective and point-of-view, don't rush to give your counter opinion. Instead, listen carefully, find areas or points for mutual agreement, and speak with love and respect.

Education is also the ability to know yourself. This is very important, my love. I can't stress this enough. You must be brutally honest with yourself to identify your strengths and weakness. You must be able to know your limitations and possibilities. Do not play or compromise your success because you failed to do the work on developing yourself and keeping a watchful eye over undeveloped areas. This can cost you greatly and can lead to major setbacks. Read books on human psychology, human behaviors, conditioning, health, and mental wellness.

I want you to know one simple fact, education does not end when you leave college. Education is a way of life. If you keep your eyes and ears open, you will learn and in turn become someone who is not only well-read and versed in the ways of knowledge, but you will also transform yourself into a more humble, kind, and loving person. Education should make us more compassionate, relatable, and giving. Knowledge is to be shared with those who have a desire to learn.

One last thing I want to share, and perhaps it is the most important one of all, the beginning of all knowledge is the fear of the Lord. You must acknowledge that everything you have and the ability to think, do and act upon comes from God as a gift to you. Not for selfish gain but for stewardship and to help others in their life journey. You must live in such a way knowing that God orders your steps. Every breath you take, and every waking moment and every sunrise and sunset has been granted by our creator.

Never let your knowledge and wisdom make you conceited or arrogant. Seek God, ask Him for wisdom, and to open your hearts and mind to understand the mysteries of life.

I promise you He will bless you beyond what you can ever imagine. I absolutely love you, my girls.

Remember,
Daddy loves you.

My prayer

Dear Lord, your Word reminds us to seek wisdom, knowledge, and understanding. My prayer for my girls is for the flame and fire of learning and education to burn constantly in their hearts. May your wisdom abound much and the desire to become scholars be used to help others and to be a voice for those who suffer in silence. May they use their gifting to bring the knowledge of Christ to all people. Thank you for their abilities, gifts, and talents. Bless my girls. Amen.

Dreams

"Dream no small dreams for they have no power to move the hearts of men."

JOHANN WOLFGANG VON GOETHE

My dearest Peanut and Chiqui,

I remember when you were both very little, perhaps around the age of three or four, you would say you have a dream of one day being someone great. A ballerina, a singer, an artist, a gymnast, a photographer, or anything your imagination was able to dream of. All those beautifully crafted dreams were perfect for your moment of desire and your mother, and I always encouraged and fueled those dreams as much as possible. After all, they were your dreams. As you both grew in age and your imaginations began to take different forms, your dreams became about something else, perhaps because you didn't see the world and your life the same way you did when you were but just a child. Either your dreams changed by the influence of external circumstances or something inside of you chose a different interest in dreams.

Dreams are important and necessary for many reasons. Quite often we think of dreams in way of images that come to us while we sleep. Dreams are like watching a movie where you are the protagonist, and the storyline revolves around you. This type of dream when everything goes well and feels wonderful awakens us to an exuberant feeling and emotion. We wake up with a sense of adventure, ready to take on anything and everything that comes our way because we feel invincible. That's the impact a wonderful dream can have on you, and it can last for the remainder of that day.

The other type of dream is of a different nature, and it requires a unique approach to achieving it and when you do, the feeling can last longer than a day, it can last a lifetime. When I hear people speak of dreams it's usually in the vein of doing or accomplishing an objective that will bring them much pleasure, fulfillment, and money. This type of dream benefits the dreamer only. Which by the way, is fine. Then, there are other types of dreamers, who see their dreams to impact, change, and empower others who are within the scope or realm of the reality of the dreamers' dream. Such was the case for Mother Theresa, Nelson Mandela, Dr. Martin Luther King, Jr., Henry Ford, Thomas Edison, and Steve Jobs, to name a few. Their dreams went beyond the scope of selfishness and grandiosity. They sought a dream that gave them a greater self of purpose, and commitment, they desire the greater good of the people and their future. A dream like that is worth having and fighting for. A dream like that is a calling.

Your dream should be so big that it frightens you when you think of achieving it. Your dream can define your life purpose and existence. It should propel you to invest all your energy, strength, thought, and lifestyle to achieve it. The dream you have should be nurtured, cared for, and protected from those who doubt your potential, ability, character, grit, discipline, and unwavering commitment to see it fulfilled. When you find your dream, define it, write it down, and post it where you can see it every day. Develop a meticulous plan on what steps you will take to achieve your dream. What are you going to need? Who are you going to seek help and mentorship from? What are you going to sacrifice? And how much is it going to cost? Remember to weigh the cost. You cannot under any circumstance begin to build your dream unless you first measure or weigh the true cost. Not just financially but, emotionally, mentally, physically, and spiritually.

As your heart wanders into a land of dreams, visions and beauty, crafted and design by the hands of the grand weaver, you will eventually come to the realization that your dreams are opportunities not just for success but for impact and change. You will need a clear and concise plan to achieve it – otherwise, your dream is just an empty wish.

The story of Joseph from the Bible is of great resource and benefit when you study it and deconstruct it. You can read about Joseph beginning in Genesis chapter 37. In the story, you will learn of a young boy who is a dreamer and how his brothers despised him for it, try to kill him, but end up selling him. Soon after, Joseph's life becomes plagued with unfortunate and painful circumstances that led to accusations and incarceration to the term of close to ten years. At the end of the story, by the miraculous work of God, Joseph ends up becoming second in command in Egypt leading the country to incredible success and fortune. Joseph had a great gift given by God to interpret dreams.

Although his own dream was a mystery to him, God allowed all unfortunate events to lead him to see his own dream become a reality. Your dreams' fulfillment may come in ways you may never imagine or suspect. However, it's important that everything you do and put your mind and hand to is done with excellence and integrity. Your life and how you conduct yourself will open doors and opportunities for you and you must be ready and prepared when they do. Your dreams, unbeknownst to you, may be a perfectly designed plan used by God to bring about significant change to the generation you live in and for future ones as well. I pray that when you hear the call for such a dream, you say *yes* and live with such purpose that nothing can discourage or stop you till you see it come to fruition. Dream big dreams my beautiful girls, the world needs your dreams and God will use them to accomplish His purpose in you.

Remember,
Daddy loves you.

My prayer

Dearest Lord, how life's most precious jewels and treasures are often the product of an accomplished dream, a desire, and vision. How often also does discouragement and fear uninvitedly walk alongside to thwart many from accomplishing their dreams. I pray Lord that you watch over my girls. Give them the courage and tenacity to overcome the obstacles that live internally. Give them strength and wisdom to stay focused and fulfill their life dreams. Amen.

Procrastination

"A little sleep, a little slumber, a little folding of the hands to rest; and poverty will come on you like a thief and scarcity like an armed man."

PROVERBS 6: 10 NIV

My dearest Peanut and Chiqui,

One of humanity's greatest villains and enemies of life is procrastination. This enemy which at times I describe as vile and diabolical has a very subtle and disguised appearance that manages to go unnoticed and undetected. Quite often it comes to us masquerading in activities and distractions. Other times it comes in ease of comfort and rest. And the most destructive and vicious way procrastination infiltrates our daily life is through trivial entertainment and amusement. Our society is numb to this reality; some even justify procrastination because they claim they have other things that are more important to take care of. The people who live a life without a plan or goal or a growth mindset will never accomplish anything worthwhile because they live life wherever the wind pushes without concern for the detrimental impact it has on them and their loved ones.

When you don't have a goal, plan, or and agenda to complete, life seems easy and passive. However, the moment you are intentional and deliberate in a specific desire or outcome, particularly in an area that can bring you much success; procrastination will invite itself and prevent you from accomplishing your goal. Procrastination has a very good track record with those who are unmotivated and who live vicariously through others. They never dare to try something new; they always speak in ways of, "One day I will, or I wish I could..." You will find these people always wanting but never doing. They will blame others and never take responsibility for their shortcomings.

Procrastination is the mother of all failures. Fail to plan or plan to fail. Be engaged and active in your work, life, and creative projects. Do not squander your greatest asset, time. Do what you need to do now. Even as you're reading this letter, go do what you intended to do this morning. Plan your life with a calendar. There is only one way of defeating procrastination, and that's by doing what you set out to accomplish. Do you remember the book *Eat That Frog* by Brian Tracy? It's a great book that speaks to the evil of procrastination and how it robs many people of their success and bright future. *Eat the ugliest and biggest frog first* was Brian Tracy's lesson. Be intentional and committed to completing your biggest task. Have a plan, put it in your calendar, keep a watchful eye for distractions that may come disguised through a phone call, text, email, appetite, people, social media, and technology. You must have a keen eye for recognizing when you are veering off task. Set a specific plan with time and dates for your goal and make it a priority and do not compromise it for anything or anyone. Do not take on too many projects at once, or the quality of your work will be compromised. Be selective about who or what you give your attention and time to, not everything and everyone deserves or should get your attention. Reduce the unnecessary clutter and chatter in your life and use your time wisely.

What I share with you about procrastination is real and destructive. I know because I have been an expert at procrastinating and leaving important things for later or another day. Procrastination has robbed me of many dreams and meaningful goals. It has stolen moments and days from my family, career, music projects, and creative goals. I have allowed procrastination to go on too long in my life till one day I mustered enough courage to be angry enough to turn my life around.

If I don't do it now, and if it's not important to me, it will never get done and no one is going to do it for me. You must develop the discipline to identify when procrastination is creeping in and overcome the temptation of giving in. Don't! Fight it off and stay focused on the task at hand. I promise you, if you discipline your life to eliminate procrastination, you will live a more peaceful fulfilled and accomplished life.

Do not put off for tomorrow what you can do today, tomorrow is not promised, and you don't know what other unnecessary distractions will appear to keep deterring you from accomplishing your given task.

One last thought. When developing your relationship with God, you will encounter many distractions that will draw your attention away. Distractions are like little minions whose sole purpose is to prevent you from your objective without making your feel guilty about putting things off for another day.

You must, at all costs, put in your calendar, time for prayer, reading God's Word, and meditating on your relationship with Him. Wake up early in the morning to spend time in solitude to reflect, ponder, and hear His voice. When He speaks, you must be still and listen. Creating a new healthy habit is difficult, but worth your time and effort.

I promise you my beautiful girls when you begin to kill and bury procrastination, you will feel more in control of your time and life; you will feel alive!

Remember,
Daddy loves you.

My prayer

Dear Heavenly Father, what is this thing called procrastination that holds many from living and being all they can be. What is it about procrastination that is enticing; luring many through its vicious ruse to abandon all reasons, logic, and commitment to completing a given task. It's as if procrastination has one goal only, to delay our process long enough till we forget and abandon our task. How subtle yet cruel and merciless procrastination can be. It mocks us and taunts us from afar patiently waiting for its next victim. I pray you awaken my girls and show them the havoc, severity, and undeniable impact this demon can have in the life of people and the atrocities it commits daily on the lives of those walking aimlessly through life. Keep my girls, I pray. Show them never to entertain or flirt with procrastination. Amen.

Religion

"If anyone among you thinks he is religious and does not bridle his tongue but deceives his own heart, this one's religion is useless. Pure and undefiled religion before God and the Father is this: to visit orphans and widows in their trouble, and to keep oneself unspotted from the world."

JAMES 1:26, 27 NIV

My dearest Peanut and Chiqui,

As I attempt to write about religion, its function and purpose in society, know that the lens by which I share comes from observation and life experiences that have collectively led me to understand and express my view of such delicate matter as is that of religion. Religion is perhaps the oldest form of an organized institution in all of humanity. Religion, as we see it and understand it today, has had many modifications and amendments to reflect the culture, the people, and its time.

There is currently an estimate of 4,300 religions in the world and that number is predicted to increase in the decades to come. But what is it about religion that is alluring and intriguing? What does religion offer humanity that seems to appeal to the mind and heart? I guess we must define religion for the purpose of clarity and understanding on what religion is. Religion according to Merriam-Webster is, *As the service and worship of god or supernatural.*

I have a different take on this, and it's based on the concept that religion is a means by which people from all walks of life attempt to create a moral system by which to devout or commit their lives to someone or something greater than themselves through rituals, service, devotion and/or ordinance for the atonement of sin. This is a common thread found in many if not all religions of the world. A particular code of conduct is required, and one must identify with such religion to project an image of devotion and consecration to illustrate a lifestyle.

Religion throughout the ages has had a wonderful and much-needed impact on the lives of its followers and it has also created a moral code of conduct to preserve and protect its parishioners and communities from personal and collective demise. There is beauty in religion and much to honor and respect. However, the aspect of religion that some people abhor and deliberately detest is that religion is viewed and seemed like an oppressive system that marginalizes and discriminates against those who do not have or share the same view. In many cultures and countries around the world, religion plays a major role on the laws created and passed. Systems are designed to preserve the beliefs of the majority of the dominating religion but do not favor those who do not practice it. Currently, in this present generation there is such contempt for religion as it's portrayed negatively, regressive, antiquated, and discriminating.

Perhaps people do have a viable reason for feeling such disgust toward religion. After all, many wars have been fought in the name of religion. Many people throughout history have been murdered, ostracized, tortured, and incarcerated for not following or submitting to a particular religious belief system. This seems very unfair and inhumane. Look back in history and you will see that religion has always been at the core of government, laws, wars, education, money, taxes, monuments, statutes, and civic order.

As you begin your search on all religions of the world and particularly the major ones, you will find common threads among all of them. Religion requires faith in someone greater than yourself, such as God or a supernatural force or being. Religion requires repentance, penance, and devotion to structures, rituals, rites, and obligations. For many people throughout the world, this is a way of life, they don't know anything else. Many are life practitioners who were birth into a certain religion and don't have any other paradigm by which to live or see the world.

As you traverse this beautiful world we live in, you will come in contact with people from all walks of life and religions. You have the responsibility to learn as much as you can about a particular belief system before you cast your solicited or unsolicited opinion. You must learn to listen closely, attentively, respectfully, and carefully to why people believe what they believe and why they choose to follow and serve a particular religion. Our duty is not to pass judgment but observe and respect people for their views.

I would be remiss if I did not mention or forewarn you of the danger religion can also have on those who practice it and are in power or a place of leadership. The human heart is a mystery, an abyss and at times an enigma. Who can ever decipher the deep matters of the heart? A person who is a devout believer and practitioner must accept the responsibility to never usurp and misuse power to destroy another person's life. In theory, the intent of every major religion is to make us better humans, willing and eager to serve our neighbors and make humanity better – to draw closer to our Creator or deity and become better people.

My advice to you is before you commit yourself to anything or anyone; particularly a religious belief system, do enough research on it. Consider and weigh the cost of commitment. For religion will ask for your life. Make an informed decision if you choose to follow and serve and consider if it's worth following. Perhaps the greatest thought on religion is that it can serve a higher purpose in the world and life only when its theoretical application is greater than its messengers.

Remember,
Daddy loves you.

My prayer

Dearest Father, oh how Jesus fought with many religious zealots of His time. How He exposed them of their tyranny, abuse, manipulation, injustice, and corruption toward those they claimed to serve. The truest religion you ask us is to love God our Father with all our heart, mind, and soul and to love our neighbor-brother. May my beautiful girls understand that religion if not vetted properly and analyzed closely can claim life and destroy it. The very core of religion is the ability to exercise self-control and tame the tongue. May the truest and purest aspect of who the girls will be, mirror the very image of God. Amen.

The Church

"In the same way the Church exists for nothing else but to draw men into Christ, to make them little Christs. If they are not doing that, all the cathedrals, clergy, missions, sermons, even the Bible itself, are simply a waste of time."

C.S. LEWIS

Dearest Peanut and Chiqui,

The topic of the church is very dear to my heart, for I, like many others in ancient times as well as today have struggled to understand how something that is at times so dysfunctional as is the church, has lasted for over two thousand years. It's puzzling and bewildering to see the church outlive its pallbearers. So much good and bad can be said about the church and its representatives. Throughout history, the church has played a significant role in establishing itself as the ultimate authority of all things moral and appointees of God's grace and mercy. However, if you look closely, for over two thousand years the church has made significant blunders and atrocities all in the name of God, moreover to many of its close followers and servants, the sword had not been spared.

The Greek word for church is *called out ones*. We read in Matthew 16:18, where Jesus said, "*And I also say to you that you are Peter and on this rock I will build My church.*" Jesus again mentioned the church in Matthew 18:17. However, the birth of the actual church happened during Pentecost (Acts 2:1-4) when the Holy Spirit descendent upon all who were gathered there. They were filled with the Holy Spirit. This event led to the early years of the church. The early apostles had the enormous task and responsibility to lay the foundation for the *called out ones* to begin a new life found in Christ. The people who believed in Jesus began to be taught and learn discipleship in their newfound faith. Peter, who once denied Jesus three times, became the orator to declare the good news, which is the gospel.

The early church was very peculiar and special because they actually lived and practiced a way of life that illustrated all that Jesus had done. They were called Christians because they actually lived and acted like Christ. They became true representatives and ambassadors of Jesus. They were an expression of God's love, kindness, and benevolence to all they came in contact. They helped each other financially and they supported one another with charity, alms and were authentically generous in the support for those in need. The early believers or the *call out one's* primary focus was to meet the basic and spiritual needs in their communities. To reach those who were in spiritual darkness by bringing a message of hope, healing, and salvation.

The evidence of their newfound faith and relationship with Christ was shown in the way they treated each other and how they consistently demonstrated God's love and mercy to all they came in contact with. It must be noted as well that the disciples and early believers were persecuted, murdered, imprisoned, and tortured for believing and preaching about Jesus. The early church or *called out ones* suffered greatly but loved lavishly.

I wanted to share a very concise version of the early beginnings of the church to show you how believers in Jesus' time sacrificed their lives to share the message of hope, love, forgiveness, and redemption. Believing in Jesus came with a heavy price, but they saw themselves worthy of such death, for what they had seen and believed to be, was much greater than the momentary suffering they experienced. The church or *called out ones* have a great responsibility to live a life of faith and commitment to the virtues and values Jesus preached and called His followers to do.

The life of Jesus is recorded throughout the four Gospels in the New Testament, Matthew, Mark, Luke, and John. However, the story of the all-loving and merciful God who constantly illustrates His love and affection for His creation is found throughout the entire Bible. Jesus is the completion and the true representation of God. Study the life of Christ and you will know God the Father.

So, what happened to the church? It's been over two thousand years now and the church is still here. Why? The church has survived primarily because the church belongs to God. Jesus called the church His bride. Throughout centuries and millennia, many church leaders have implemented new theological interpretations given the church a new direction, often leading away the *called out ones* to new theories, philosophical perspectives, and loose concepts of the duty and function of the church in society. Moreover, as time passed, the world became more populated, new religions were birthed, the world expanded, new inventions and discoveries opened a new way of looking at life and the world.

Sciences and the arts blossomed, philosophers and thinkers gave their unsolicited opinion as facts and truths, many making claims that God is dead and there's no need to believe or fear Him anymore. Technology has made life easier, convenient, and yet more complex. Education took the place of faith, and the church grew cold in their love for God and their fellow brother.

The church eventually became another institution that was seen by some as a failed and narrow-minded way of living. Many wars have been fought in the name of God, much abuse of power and tyranny has plagued the church through centuries. Many parishioners have suffered sexual abuse from priests and church leaders. Corruption has also done great damage. The church today stands on ideas and methods that are highly questionable in its practices in order to compete with secularism and appease the masses.

In spite of all of this, I truly believe deep in my heart that the church, the *called out ones*, belong to God.

History has shown us that generations go from chaos to order and from order to chaos. This is seen throughout all humanity and God has always spoken to every generation. The church in and of itself is dysfunctional because it's led by imperfect people. This behavior, however, is not excused as God will bring all our deeds and actions into judgment on our final day. We will all have to give an account for all we've done in this life.

I want you to know one last thing. I've had a very contentious relationship with the church and its leaders. I have suffered greatly at the hand of many of the so-called oracles and men and women of God. I stand here writing this letter, solely and only because of the grace and mercy of God and I believe He has called me and kept me to be a voice for such a time as this. I have learned that I too am part of the church, and I must choose if I'm going to be a true representative of God's love and forgiveness in this world or continue to misrepresent Christ.

We are "called out ones" we are to live a life truly vested and committed to Christ. The church is not a building nor a temple; we, humans are the church, we are His bride, and we have a calling to be of such character and beauty so the unbeliever can see God's love in us. I love you, my girls. And my message to you is to love the church because you are the church. Be the *called out ones* God has chosen for this generation to be a light and a beacon of hope and love.

Remember,
Daddy loves you.

My prayer

Dearest Father, I pray you watch over my girls, and you teach them to guard their hearts. May they live committed to you and your message for this world. I pray they may clearly and undeniably understand that they are the church and the institution of the church although it has its purpose, often is not an accurate representation of Christ. I pray my girls will live the gospel, the good news to serve the orphan and the widow, and to comfort those who need your touch. May their hearts never grow cold in their service to the body, your bride. Amen.

God

"What comes into our minds when we think about God is the most important thing about us."

A.W. TOZER

My dearest Peanut and Chiqui,

To the world, the existence of God has always been in question and on trial. Man has tried through the ages and through various means and philosophical ideas argue to prove that God does not exist. Furthermore, there are some who claim that the world does not need God because we're all inherently good people who unfortunately make poor choices – sometimes. The question to ask is why every generation has tried to eradicate the existence of God? What erroneous conclusions have many drawn about God? The true essence of such questions asked by many is perhaps obscure because they conceal a matter only the heart can see and know.

Every religion in the world has some sort of way of identifying something or someone as a deity, elevating it, and regarding it as holy and unequal. And then, there are some who say they don't have a religion or believe in anything. These wonderful people are mistaken because with that very statement that they don't believe in anything, is a belief in itself.

So many books and stories have been written about God. There are books on who He is and what He is. I have read great literature on God, and I have studied many scholarly essays on the matter of God. The Bible itself is a wonderful love story of a loving God who constantly demonstrates His love and affection toward humanity, but humanity because of sin always rebels and forgets about God. One of the great mysteries of the Christian faith is free will and how it not only determines our way of life but our eternal abode.

I will add that one of the most difficult things for me to acknowledge is to conclude that religion is not a true representation of God and His plan for humanity. God does not need religion to preach His message. In fact, at times I think religion does a very poor job of obeying and accomplishing what God has commanded to do. This is evident in all religions of the world; Christianity is not exempt.

Trying to explain who God is or what He is becomes an unrealistic task. Even the most scholarly person with all the research and knowledge will still come short, an infinite number of times short of who God really is. We don't have the language or capacity to truly know or fully comprehend this great mystery. However, my desire is to share with you, what I have learned through my study and life experiences to be consistent and evident for me.

Throughout my life, I've always wondered who God is or what He is. Never fully understanding the weight of my questions, I continued to live with the notion that God somehow stays in the background of life. A behind-the-scenes kind of God, who looks over me and although all-powerful, yet allows things to go on as if He has nothing to say about my life choices. My belief in God has always been distant and, if truth be told, lukewarm. I never truly or fully committed to knowing Him or having a meaningful relationship with Him. Only recently, I came to see that my perception through the lens or paradigm I lived my life, had blurred the reality of who God has always been and what He really is. When I mustered enough courage to get rid of *religion* and seek God for myself and search the Bible thoroughly, I then began to see the great mystery that appears to be elusive and ensnared or trapped in religion.

It was as if someone was intentionally leading my heart and eyes to a hidden reality that God has been more than a God in the background, that God is not aloof.

God has always been and will always be present in every aspect of life. Based on my life experience and everything I learned from history, literature, the Bible, and teachers, and through much observation, I have concluded that God is extremely merciful toward His creation. He will never relent from showing His mercy and grace to all of us. His mercy is in response to the love He has for you and me. God is good, He is love, He is forever kind, and He will never withhold any of His beautiful attributes from His children. God is all-knowing. He knows all our thoughts and every single second and minute of our lives. His knowledge of us is perfect, He is aware of every good and bad thing that will happen to us. He knows every thought and action before we do it. He knows what will happen ten years from now. God is never worried or overwhelmed by what happens on earth. God is perfect. God is complete. Another concept that is very difficult for humanity to grasp is that God is eternal. He is not limited by time or space. He was not created by someone greater than Himself. He lives in eternity. He does not have a beginning nor an end.

As you continue to live your life, you will come to many crossroads and forks in the road for which you will need to decide which way to travel. Your life choices will lead you down new paths and adventures. Keep your eyes and ears open to the great mystery that God is. You will find God in the eyes of a homeless person, you will find God in a refugee, in a hungry child, in a forgotten widow, or an elderly woman in her dying days. You might also find God in solitude or in a quiet, peaceful breeze. You might find

God in the laughter of a child, or the tears of the broken-hearted.

Do not assume to find God in temples made of stone, where cold hearts and distant, shadowy eyes dwell in judgment. God lives in you. He dwells in your heart. He is with you always. He loves you, cares for you, and will be by your side always. God is not distant; He is near and present. He is your provider, keeper, protector, and Savior. God will never forsake you. He is your true heavenly father. I love you, my beautiful girls.

Remember,
Daddy loves you.

My prayer

Dear God, anything I say and pen in this letter and prayer come short to your true nature-all powerful and all-knowing. Who can ever comprehend the mind and ways of God? You truly are a mystery and as C.S. Lewis stated, "after all, He's not a tamed Lion, but He's good." Yes! You are good! I pray my girls will forever experience your goodness and see your mercy in the land of the living. May they search for you, learn from you, and live for you. In all the volumes ever written, all the art ever produced, all the wisdom in the hearts of men and women will forever come short in comparison to who You truly are. There are no words or anything we can ever imagine or utter that can be worthy of describing your nature and being. You are marvelously terrifying.

As my two beautiful girls make their way through life, they will be confronted with challenging questions and vicious attacks on their faith in You. Reveal yourself to them in such a way that nothing in this world will ever draw them from your care. I bless my girls as I ask You to keep watch over them. Bless them today and forever. Amen.

Mommy

"A wife of noble character who can find. She is worth far more than rubies...her children arise and call her blessed; her husband also and he praises her."

PROVERBS 31: 10, 28 NIV

My dearest Peanut and Chiqui,

These letters would not be complete if I did not include a letter on the most beautiful and wonderful woman – your mother. Our lives would not be what they are today if it was not for the wisdom, gentleness, patience, and love your mommy displays every day. Her care and unwavering commitment to love you girls and her ability to model a life full of virtues and character is of the highest value one can ever esteem. Your mother is the embodiment of grace, beauty, love, strength, joy, commitment, and integrity. Your mother was hand-picked by God from His lushed garden, planted in the riches soil, and illuminated by His radiant light, watered by the dew of His presence for you and for me. I am so undeserving of such a gift, but God so it fit to bestow such beauty in my life, a life that was mired in grief, sorrow, pain, and bitterness. God chose His most precious rose to bring His sweet fragrance to my life. Through your mother's life, God has shown me His goodness and abundant love.

One of the characteristics that make your mommy extraordinary is her love and devotion to God. From the first day I met her, she exuded a reverence and commitment to her heavenly father. God has always been the center of her heart and has always captivated her mind and spirit. No one else can ever take that place. She has lived her life as scrupulous and aware of His presence and has devoted her life to serve and honor Him. Her heart has always belonged to her Maker. A second characteristic that makes your mommy exceptional is her devotion to prayer.

Prayer has been her constant pillar in life. She told me once that when she was a young girl in her early teens, a youth leader told her to begin to pray for her husband and that wherever he may be, that God would begin to do a great work in his life. Since that day, your mother never stopped praying for me. And I can tell you and confirm that all the great work God has done in my life is because of your mother's prayers. She prays for our home, she prays for our family, and she especially prays for you girls, always. Even before you were each born, your mommy has never stopped praying for you and modeling a lifestyle of humility, character, modesty, kindness, meekness, integrity, and true beauty. Your mommy is the truest form of elegance and class.

Another admirable aspect of your mommy is her devotion to worship God. Not merely in music per se, but in her authenticity to reverence God for who He is, Holy. Music plays a major part in our household and as we have spoken many times, contemporary worship music is but a genre only; but that's not worship. What your mother has displayed in her life is a life of obedience, a relentless pursuit for God's presence and character. She embodies a dedicated life to servanthood and an uncompromising attitude to honor God with all of her being. That's worship. Music just becomes the expression of her heart and constant living. I completely love that about your mommy.

Your mommy is also an amazing daughter. She loves Papa and Mama. She cares for them, seeks them, calls them every day, is attentive and caring. She loves to be with them and honors them in every way possible. She makes sacrifices to ensure they are taken care of, she looks for ways to remind them they are loved and how she appreciates and is grateful for everything they did to give her a godly life, one that honors God and cares for family and friends. Papa and mama have been the foundation for who she is today, a virtuous and godly woman.

Your mommy is also a marvelous wife. She's patient, caring, loving, a great steward of her house, and full of wisdom and knowledge. Her insight into her commitment to teach and model for you God's love has been evident in our home and in your lives. She will bring you in our bed or as you girls always say, “Mommy’s bed,” and pray over you, talk with you, read the Bible with you, cry with you and constantly say how much she loves you and how proud she is of you both. Your mommy is God’s expression of heaven on earth.

I have always felt undeserving of your mommy’s beauty, tenderness, wisdom, her gentle touch, and beautiful, big brown eyes. I fell in love with, her character, passion, and undeniable relationship with God. You see my girls, my life prior to meeting your mommy was very dark, eerie, and troubled. Broken, shattered, and rejected. But God saw it fit to give me as a gift a precious angel as my partner, wife, and the mother of my two darlings. Your mother has modeled with her life, in the good times and bad, to what a godly woman should do and be.

You will eventually grow older and have your own families with husbands and kids. Marriage is beautiful, exquisite, and precious and at times extremely painful, difficult, and daunting. However, your mommy has been a true trailblazer in her relentless commitment to God, prayer, worship, and her family, and especially to you princesses. Honor your mother, show her your love. Esteem her for all of her beauty and wisdom. Imitate her patience, kindness, character, and integrity. Honor her with your life and all your affection. As your mommy always says, “As long as you make God the center of your marriage, He will order your steps... remember the Lord is always with you." I love you so much.

Remember,
Daddy loves you.

My prayer

Dear Lord, words can never express my gratitude and appreciation for the wife you have gifted me. Her strength, wisdom, courage, love, patience, compassion, and godly character have been the staples for our marriage and foundation. Her tender words and gentle touch have always inspired me to be the man you called me to be. Her prayers over me have kept me from my own demise. Thank you, Lord, for she has been an incredible mother who seeks constantly the well-being of her girls, a model of modesty, beauty and humility. I pray my heavenly Father that as my girls grow older, that they may remember the example, their mother has been, and may they imitate her lifestyle and commitment to be a virtuous woman in an ever-compromising world. May your word be a lamp unto their feet and may the husbands they will select as a life partner be ever in your care and molding. I bless my girls and their future life in motherhood. Amen.

Final Letter

"Never compromise integrity for comfort."

-E.RUSTRIAN

My dearest Peanut and Chiqui,

This is my final letter to you, my precious girls. I have shared so much concerning life, God, finances, relationships, and virtues. I share them as pearls because I have lived through some of the most challenging seasons where I experienced tragedy, pain, and setbacks. But through it all, I have learned to see each experience not independently from all others, but as a tapestry or a canvas of great artistic prowess by our endowed Creator. He draws beauty from ashes. All these life experiences can only be seen as a life well-lived.

You may be asking yourselves how I can possibly say such a thing considering all I've experienced. I learned that I am responsible for the choices I make, and I must take responsibility for my actions. I made poor decisions, but in the end, I learned and I've become a better man. A better father and a better husband. Other unfortunate experiences were out of the realm of my control. They came from people who made poor choices, who themselves were in a bad place. My dear girls, God has given us the right to choose how we want to live life and what to do in life. I chose to let go and forgive all those who hurt me, including family members. I chose to also forgive myself and see that God has taken my mistakes, sorrow, anger, and inner turmoil and given me joy, peace, and serenity.

You will eventually realize that all these things I wrote to you are connected and that they are not isolated. You will have to make tough decisions, and at times your integrity and character will be tested. Your moral compass will be tried and your faith in God will be questioned and often mocked and ridiculed. You must choose a path, and once you have done so, commit your hand to the work that lies ahead. Don't be lazy or become distracted. Stay focused and determined to live a life well-lived. Don't be afraid, be courageous, don't live in doubt, but live in faith and above all, live fearlessly.

Live a life full of gratitude, humility, joy, peace, and passion. Forgive as often as possible, love beyond your comfort, be kind to those who encounter you, give generously, think of others, celebrate the goodness and wonder of humanity, love, and forgive yourself. Don't look at your failures as the end, see them as opportunities to become masters at living and defeating a doubtful mindset. Discipline your life and life will reward you for it.

For as long as God gives me health and strength I will be by your side, patiently waiting for our next talk, our next adventure, our next moment. I will walk alongside of you to cheer you on, to pray and encourage you when things get tough, to hear you when you're angry or hurting, to listen intently when you disagree with me, or when you are ready to fly on your own.

I will always love you. I will always cherish every moment we spent together, every tear we cried, and every time we shared laughter. You will forever be my princesses, and nothing will ever change that. As your father, I will do my best to continue to grow, read more books on how to become a better father, and continue to be the father you need. Never forget how much I love you. Forever your daddy...forever, my Peanut and Chiqui.

Remember,
Your daddy loves you. Always!

My prayer

Dearest Lord, my heart is full and at peace. You have blessed me beyond my wildest dreams. You have changed the trajectory of my family and future generations and You have shown so much mercy toward me and my family. I live in complete awe and gratitude for how you love. This simple prayer is to say thank You for saving me, thank You for keeping me. Thank You for all the life lessons that have taught me to love, forgive, care and give. You truly are the Father to the fatherless. Please watch over my girls. And although I know they will need to go through life's toughest valleys, may they remember the Good Shepherd will keep them in perfect peace. I bless my girls and may they never part from your will and the purpose for which they were created, to honor and worship You. Thank you, Father! Amen.

This book is comprised of real letters I've written for my two amazing daughters, and up till now, you've been reading my interactions with them. Now, dear reader, I'm respectfully addressing you.

Thank you for coming on this intimate, personal journey with us. If there is any way that I can serve you, perhaps speak at your church, to married couples, or to fathers and/or mothers, or to speak to the children of your church - it would be my honor and pleasure. As a lifelong educator, teaching, especially life-changing content like this is one of my great joys.

I'm also available to be a guest on your show; Radio, Television, YouTube, or Podcast. If parents from any walks of life listen or watch your show, I believe I can provide life and good counsel through God's word.

I can be reached at the following:

Website: www.erustrian.com
Instagram: @edvinrustrian

May God bless you and watch over your family.

May your daughters grow to be amazing, self-assured women that love themselves, understand their value, and love God. May they make you proud and add worth (and maybe sparkles) to the family name.

ABOUT THE AUTHOR

Edvin Rustrian is an educator, accomplished author, speaker, arranger, composer, recording artist, playwright, proud father and loving husband. His passion for music and the arts are an expression of his love and dedication to God. He once again captivates the imagination of the audience by cultivating opportunities for critical thinking and search for a deeper meaning in the human experience. His life's pursuit is to live a life full of gratitude and purpose.

As I begin this new journey my desire and focus in writing this book is to share my heart on topics such as faith, fatherhood, family, education, literature, philosophy, the arts, values, purpose and all things related to deep thinking. However, if you ask me, out of all those things, what matters the most to me? I would say two things: One, loving God with all my heart. My relationship with God is the most important relationship I will ever have. It's where my identity is grounded. Second, fatherhood. There is such a need for fathers and for their presence in the home. We are living in a fatherless generation and we need to sound the alarm. Children need their fathers, wives need their husbands, communities need men to take their God-given place.

Learn more at ERustrian.com

www.erustrian.com | Instagram: @edvinrustrian